DON'T LIKE THE WAY IT IS?
CHANGE IT!

DON'T LIKE THE WAY IT IS? CHANGE IT!

Changing Before Or After An Ultimatum

K.L. Fischer PhD

K.L. Fischer Publications

Publisher: K.L. Fischer Publications

ISBN-13: 978-1533491282
ISBN-10: 1533491283

Table of Contents

"To Need Is To Be Weak" Is A Delusion Held By
Those Who Would Be Strong

Coping With The Vagaries And Realities Of Everyday
Life – Therapy Can Help

The Don't Likes In Our Lives

Anxiety Can Be A Precipitator For Changing

Changing Can Be A Precipitator For Anxiety

Changing Begins With Ourselves! What Changes Are
We Willing To Make?

Changing Within The Context Of Our Primary
Relationship

Assertiveness Holds The Key To Changing
Perceptions Of Ourselves

"Good Luck" In Changing The Other!

What Characteristics Of The Other Are Resistant To
Change?

What's Been Happening To You In The Company Of
The Other?

Deal Breakers

Giving The Other An Ultimatum, What Makes It So
Hard?

What Do You Do? (The One Giving The Ultimatum)

What The Other Needs To Do

The One Getting The Ultimatum, What Is It Like For Them?

What Are They Like If They're Starting To Get It?

What Is The One Who Gave The Ultimatum Looking For From The Other?

When Is Enough Not Enough?

What If The One Giving The Ultimatum Gets A <u>No Way</u> From The Other?

As A Therapist I Wish Both Had Come To Me Sooner

The Saddest Scenario Of All

Rationalization As A Defense

My Message To You My Reader

"To Need Is To Be Weak" Is A Delusion Held By Those Who Would Be Strong

I don't know about you but I was brought up believing that to need was to be weak. I must have picked this up from my father, who must have made it his practice to keep his feelings to himself. Maybe he showed them now and then to my older sister, but the only feeling of his that has stayed in my long-term memory was his anger when he felt out of control of what was happening around him. His face, his voice, his gestures left no doubt in my mind as to what he was feeling at the time. The one thing I learned very early on was you didn't want to make him angry. If you did, all hell broke loose. To this day I still don't know for sure why I didn't more often run for cover. Maybe I was already putting the need not to appear weak to my father higher than the need to protect myself from the fallout of his rantings. Hadn't he told me early on to take my medicine like a little soldier; that crying wouldn't get me anywhere; to take my hands away and take my punishment like a little man.

"To need is to be weak." Over the thirty-five years I've been a practicing psychologist, I literally can't count the number of clients I've seen who must have had this drummed into their heads (as words to live by) from their childhood on; and, as a consequence of this, felt very hesitant and uncomfortable about seeing me (at first) and giving me the perception they needed help. Add to this group, those people who thought about the possibility of coming to see me but couldn't bring themselves to do it because they didn't want to appear weak before a "father figure." And finally, add the people who were in denial about needing help because their need not to see themselves as weak was well defensed and kept them in the dark about their need for help.

I'm going to do my damnedest to be a counter-propagandist and try to convince you, naysayers, otherwise. I say to need is part of being human.

Certainly, where survival needs are concerned you would agree. To have needs that go beyond our survival needs is to want more for ourselves than just to physically survive. We need more of a purpose in life than merely to physically survive. I'm not implying with the word "merely" that physical survival isn't absolutely vital to our existence but I am implying there's much more involved when we allow ourselves to think purposefully about our <u>essence</u> as well as our <u>existence</u>.

Our essence — who we are; why we were put here; what our purpose is; what makes our life meaningful...These questions can be addressed from a theological, philosophical, or psychological perspective. Actually, all three contribute to our understanding of life and our place and purpose in it.

You're probably wondering where is he going with this. Isn't this going to take us away from the subject of needing i.e. needing more than what it takes to survive physically (albeit that for many of us it would seem that surviving physically takes up an inordinate, disproportionate amount of time and energy in our everyday lives).

When one grows up holding fast to the idea that needing is a sign of weakness, they tend to ask for no quarter nor give any either. The thinking behind this is

– If I don't ask for any help, I don't have to give any either.

There are some who are into giving help but don't ask for help. I wonder what's really going on here. Some of these same people when one offers to help them, refuse it, even if the truth were told they could really use it. Maybe, we're talking about to-need-is-to-be-weak kind of people here. What happens to these people is that eventually they get tired of giving to others and helping others and (so it seems to them) getting so little in return, that their giving and helping slows down and in some cases even dries up.

I can understand why they might end up feeling like they do – Too much was going out from them and too little was coming back to them. But, in a way, they brought this disparity of giving and receiving, outgoing vs. incoming upon themselves. Part of the reason it turned out for them the way it did is because their need to be perceived as strong was greater than their need to ask for or receive help.

Another thing that could be going on with these people is that in giving to people what they're asking for, the giver gains some control of the other, and conversely, if they were to ask for help and receive that help from the other, they'd feel like they're giving away control of themselves to the other.

These people, I've been referring to as to-need-is-to-be-weak kind of people, who feel like they're losing some control when they let others help them, I get excited about, when (for whatever the reason) they decide to come see me.

I can relate to what it took for them to acknowledge they could use some help. They had to fight hard against the kind of thinking they had been brought up with to reach this point.

It took me until my early thirties to admit to myself I needed help. Up to that point, true to my upbringing, I had been trying to do it all myself. I needed that much to be in control. I needed that much to perceive myself, and be perceived by others, as not needing help and being strong and self-sufficient. But I also, thankfully, came to realize it was all becoming too much for me. I was angry and agitated and depressed most of the time.

I later came to realize one of the main reasons it seemed like no one was there to help me was because I became angry with myself about needing help and angry at others for not offering it. But think about it. Who wants to be around and give help to an angry person who's angry about needing help and receiving it.

I sought help at the time by joining group therapy led by a husband (psychiatrist) and his wife, (psychologist) – as co-therapists. For the first couple of months my resistance toward receiving help was high – That plus my tendency to intellectualize kept the group at bay from getting at my feelings. But the group members were not to be denied. They got around my head to my heart. I became more open as I realized my angry defenses couldn't drive them away. Once I became open, they gave, and I received. I had to go on alone no more and felt stronger for it.

Each of us needs to find their purpose in this life. If we are spiritually-minded we hold fast to the belief God has a plan for us. Some of us say – Yah, but He hasn't revealed it to us – yet. Or, it could just as well be the case He's been revealing it to us, (here and there), only we haven't perceived it as such – Not yet anyway. Again whether we get theological, philosophical, or psychological about our life the questions remain the same while the answers may be different.

Coping With The Vagaries And Realities Of Everyday Life – Therapy Can Help

Life is a process that is on-going. It doesn't wait for us to figure things out. We have our hands and hearts full just trying to cope with the vagaries and realities of everyday life: – The never knowing what's going to happen next. Life playing out according to Murphy's Law. The emotional rollercoaster ride. The struggle to keep one's head about water. The frustration of falling further behind. The sudden illnesses. The unexpected losses. The one step forward and two steps back. The paying the bills. The not paying the bills. The unavoidable having a bad day. The stressors of being together, of drifting apart; and so on [You go ahead and add your own realities to my list].

Is it any wonder then by the time my client comes to see me, especially those I've been seeing for a while and therefore feel very comfortable with me, they plunk themselves down in their chair and for the first and probably the last time in their day, they can take some deep breaths, slouch down a bit, and let someone be for them for a change, who accepts them as they are.

There's no agenda to deal with. There is no expectation to meet. They don't have to talk if they don't want to. Sometimes, it's enough just to sit in silence and enjoy the quietude with someone who cares about you. One doesn't have to be an expert in person perception (although I am, he says humbly) to see they had a bad day. They've come to the right place; I hope they know that.

I do have clients though who when they've been having a bad day decide at the end of the day to cancel coming; Or, if they've been having a rough week so far and are out of sorts (as they put it) they will call and ask me if they still should come; Or, when they haven't been able to follow through with something I encouraged them to try (and they had said they would) they cancel and tell me the next time why they didn't come.

My dear clients sometimes turn things on their head – Their way of thinking keeps them from getting what they need. They're depressed. They're anxious.

They're frustrated. They're feeling they let me down, let themselves down. They're tired of carrying the load. They don't feel appreciated. They've got way too much on their plate. They're not getting enough help. There's too much for one person. They want to quit but they can't. They're very unhappy but they're stuck.

So what do they do. You'd think they would leap at the chance to be with someone who will listen to them vent; empathize with their situation; support them; encourage them; give them helpful insights; and essentially give them a place and opportunity to unload what's weighing them down and pick up in their place something that will make their burdens in life lighter to carry.

What some of my clients do, especially those who still subscribe to – "To need is to be weak" is – They start coming up with excuses not to come on a regular basis. Or they'll want to come once a month and they cancel that appointment. Or they'll say they don't need it anymore. Or they'll just stop coming, period.

We need to take a closer look at factors determining whether people will opt for therapy in the first place, or whether, if they do come, they will stay with it. Firstly, there is the realization they don't like the way things are going in their life. They have needs (they may not know what they are yet) that are not being met. This may be making them anxious or depressed, or both. They describe it as an overall feeling of being unhappy. Here we've come to a critical choice point in these people's lives. The key to whether they will opt for therapy or not is whether they see themselves at this junction deserving more from life than they're getting. Do they deserve to be happy? Or do they deserve to be unhappy? If the answers are Yes, No, the chances are fair to good they'll look into therapy.

Once they come to therapy, they usually need to be assured by me that I understand how big a step they've taken just to come. My privilege is to give them the overall feeling they've come to the right place and the right person. I will listen well to what they have to say. I will listen to the music behind their words to help them uncover their feelings trapped within them. By their self-report and my observations I will discern how they see themselves and feel about themselves. I will also get a pretty good picture of how they see others see them; and how they see the others in their lives.

When we get to the point in therapy where I ask them what they need there's usually silence, presumably as they think about it. Their body language is telling me some of them (at least) haven't given it much thought (if any) before. Most of them, when they recover enough to speak, come up with what I would have predicted, an "I don't know."

The Don't Likes In Our Lives

Early in their therapy (unbeknownst to them), they are telling me what they need to change or be changed, when they're relating to me what they <u>don't like</u> about what's going on in their lives. What we <u>need to</u> happen in our lives is the antithesis of what we <u>need not to</u> happen, or <u>don't like it</u> when it does happen in our lives.

For example, the way this works is my client doesn't like how poorly they are treated at work, in particular by their employer – That's, what's been happening to them – That's, what they don't like happening to them – That's, what they need not to be happening to them. What they need from me are insights about themselves, about their employer, about the perceptions each is giving and receiving from the other, along with a generous supply of empathy for what it must be like to be going through what they're going through.

It works this way for other things that have been happening to my clients that they don't like. Here's a sampling of their concerns about <u>what they don't like</u>

that are happening in their lives: They don't like their other is distancing themselves from them. They don't like the breakdown in their communication. They don't like that the people at their other's workplace see more of them than they do. They don't like that they haven't gone out together, just the two of them, but once in the past six months. They don't like the tone of their child's voice and what the child has to say when talking back to them.

They don't like that their life seems so much to be out of their control. They don't like that they can't remember the last time they had any fun. They don't like the feeling they're not appreciated and are taken for-granted. They don't like that their life seems to consist of sameness and routine. They don't like that their life seems consumed by the roles they play, and that they don't have a clue what they need as a person. They don't like that they're afraid to try new things. They don't like that they tend to overreact to things, catastrophize what happens to them. They don't like that they don't have a friend they can trust. They don't like that people are always coming to them with their problems, but won't listen to theirs without interrupting. They don't like that they work their head off but get little thanks for it. They don't like that when they wake up in the morning they wish the day were over before it gets started. They don't like the feeling they have at the end of the day that they didn't accomplish anything. They don't like the fact that no matter how hard they work they can't get ahead, hell, they can't even stay even. They don't like that they don't give a damn anymore about how they look, they used to, but they don't anymore. They don't like that they're growing old, time is flying by, and they've missed out on so much of their life they do like.

As before, go ahead and add your own I don't likes to my list. But, be advised, my reader, if you take this upon yourself (as I hope you will do, preferring that it be in the context of therapy) to think about what you don't like about your life, you may discover early on you'd like to add this exercise to your list of I don't likes. ☹ Our defenses tend to steer us away from looking objectively and realistically at what we don't like about our lives. We're afraid if we "go there" we might open Pandora's Box and out may come a plethora of I don't likes.

Isn't it intrinsically a downer for us to think about what we don't like about our life. What will happen to us if once we get started our list becomes too long? Won't this bring us even further down than we are already? Shouldn't we rather focus on what we <u>do like</u> about our life? And even though this list may be shorter, at least we'll feel better about it!

I'm asking you to trust me on this (Remember I did say it would be better if you did this in the context of therapy).

I think the main reason our defenses don't want us to think about the I don't likes in our life is because they want to spare us the anxiety and depression they are sure will come if we think about our I don't likes, find ourselves dwelling on them and, where the real downer comes in, see no way to change them.

I said earlier that people (although they may not realize it at the time) are telling me what they need to change, or be changed, when they're relating to me what they don't like about what's going on in their lives.

Telling me what they <u>don't like</u>, (they may not realize) is like telling me what they <u>would like</u> [if things could only change].

Anxiety Can Be A Precipitator For Changing

What brings them to me in the first place, (assuming they are not coerced) is the anxiety and/or depression they are experiencing because their lives are compromised by too many don't-likes and too few do-likes. The costs far outweigh the rewards. Life has become too heavy for them. They need help. And that's what I'm here for – To give them the help they need – The kind of help that will ultimately help them help themselves to what they need.

Remember, I said before there are factors playing a significant role in determining whether people will opt for therapy in the first place – We covered that by pointing out – The I don't likes in their lives, once their defenses allow them to see them, and the anxiety and depression that accompany them bring them to me. But, whether once they come, they stay a while in therapy depends upon whether are able to identify what they need (Need sounds too much like need as in survival) i.e. what they would <u>like their life to be like</u> if they were able to change some of the I don't likes into I do likes and add some new ones.

Some people (maybe you're one of them) look at the I don't likes going on in their lives, shrug their shoulders, and present like they've already dismissed them out of hand. It's like they're saying (without saying it) that's the way life goes. There's nothing they can do about it. What's the use of thinking about it being any different. They'll only get more frustrated, and for what.

As a reality therapist, I look at the realities of their life with them. They are telling me by their facial expression, their mannerisms, their tone, the content of their words how they perceive the life they're living; and the people in it; how they think others perceive them; how they perceive themselves. Their perceptions are their reality. I need to get as close as I can to perceiving their reality, while staying grounded with my own perceptions of their perceptions. Empathy does not require as a prerequisite we "walk in the other's shoes" (we couldn't if we tried) but to come as close as we can to feeling what they're feeling "walking in their shoes."

I give my clients the insight that they're telling me (without telling me) what they would like to see happen in their life when they've told me already what they haven't liked happening in their life. So their litany of I don't likes serves a beneficial purpose, albeit it may seem to them a monologue of cynicism and negativity. Sometimes our thinking works this way. Needing to think first of the negative i.e. what we don't like about our life; then talking to someone who can be objective, empathize with us, accept our perceptions as being real to us, and make no value judgments.

[Of course, I give them the opportunity and encourage them to use therapy to share with me what they do like about what's going on in their life, as well.]

Are you a bit surprised I've put the I don't likes before the I do likes. I've done it this way because that's how it usually goes in therapy. I guess it's fair to say if my prospective client had a lot of I do likes and just a few I don't likes, they probably wouldn't be coming to see me (although an exception to this would be a case in which it wasn't quantity that mattered but quality. Meaning the prospective client weighted more heavily the few I don't likes than the many I do likes.

Were a client to come to see me who presented, from my perspective, a ridiculously rosy picture, I would probably conclude they were up to the ears in defenses, or, their personality was dominated by grandiosity and/or euphoria. This isn't a stretch to see them this way when you think about it. Why else would they be here. If their perception matched up with that picture of objective reality, there would be no need to come. Anxiety and/or depression emanating from their perceptions of the realities of their life and their sense of how well or poorly they are doing in life, to others, others to them, life to them – this is what brings them to me – the stressors, the stresses of life, making it harder and harder to cope, bring them to me.

They give me their self-report; they tell me what they don't like about their life, about their other, about themselves. I let them know what I'm perceiving; I give them insights about themselves and their other. Together we try to figure out what they need. Then comes the part in their therapy where, assuming the anxiety and/or depression they first brought with them has abated some, one would think they might be ready to take the next step in their therapy. That they would have seen this coming and be at least slightly prepared for it. One would like to think so. But the reality is that their therapy can be rolling right along. They've told me what they don't like. We figured out together what they would like to happen. Okay (Then I say to them): You and I have a pretty good idea about how you would like things to go in your life. Now, then, what do you think you can do to make this happen. You now know what you'd like. You have insights now about what would need to <u>change</u>. [There's that word; I said it; they heard it; I'll say they heard it!] That word <u>change</u> does it to them every time. If their anxiety had been gradually going away, it starts up again, big time. The client who's been right there with me, step for step, suddenly develops a "bad rash and cold feet."

Changing Can Be A Precipitator For Anxiety

Let's not be too hard on ourselves if we fit into my client's company. It's very normal to get anxious when even thinking about the prospect of change or changing.

I like to distinguish between these two words, change and changing. <u>Change</u> I perceive as an <u>event</u>. <u>Changing</u> to me is an <u>on-going process</u>. So when I talk to my clients, and to you my reader, I'm talking about <u>the prospect and the process of changing</u>.

Changing what? Changing It. Whatever It is, for my clients, for you, for me. I've already given you a list of Its that my clients came up with under the heading of I don't likes and asked you to go ahead and come up with your own list of I don't likes – These would be examples of <u>your</u> Its. Feel free to add more that may come to your mind as you read along.

Remember my premise about what brings my clients to me in the first place – It's the anxiety and/or depression over the buildup of too many I don't likes in their lives. They bring their anxiety to me and once they trust me, share with me their perceptions of their life, their other, themselves – perceptions which include their I don't likes and the way they feel about them.

So, simplistically we could say that anxiety brings my clients to me, (Which they're experiencing despite their defenses). But over the course of therapy something they didn't expect to happen, does: A trade-off occurs they didn't count on – a swap is made – old anxiety for new anxiety – no bargain in the short-run – but in the long-run, what a deal! Now I can tell them as they stand at the threshold of changing – that anxiety produces changing; changing produces anxiety [And, they say understandably – Now, he tells me!

The prospect of the process of changing particularly makes us anxious when it becomes clear to us that we will be the ones doing the changing. We thought when our anxiety over I don't likes brought us to therapy, it would mostly be the subject or object of our I don't likes that would need to do the changing. And now it appears we are being asked to look at

24

ourselves and consider what about ourselves needs changing.

Our first response is to feel like a "bait and switch" has been pulled on us. We came to therapy because we knew this much – That our life needed changing, and felt strongly about the other needing changing. But ourselves needing changing. If we had thought about this at all, we certainly had no idea we would go first – That the bulk of our therapy would now focus on the process of changing ourselves i.e. changing our perception of ourselves; of how others perceive us, of others, (and how they perceive themselves).

I'm sure you've heard this many times before – You can't change others – The only one you can change is yourself. When one changes themselves they see things, others, life, themselves, differently. This isn't to say that because one sees differently their I don't likes go away. Some of them may. Others one may see in a different light. There will be those I don't likes that will still be seen as they were before.

Changing Begins With Ourselves!
What Changes Are We Willing To Make?

So let's talk about change and changing from the perspective of one who has accepted the proposition that if one wants their life to change and others in their life to change the changing begins with themselves. Think about your own situation and the probability you would be willing to begin the process of changing.

Let's brainstorm about what would be possible **motivators** for changing and see if any of them fit: We're tired of being tired. We're ashamed of our behavior. We feel guilty about what we did or said. We keep making the same mistakes over and over again. We don't like the way – we are, we talk, we look, we treat others. We're on a self-destructive track. Our other gave us an ultimatum. If we don't change we could die. We've been converted. We've been given another chance. [Add your own motivators to this list. My list is not intended to be complete.]

What about **obstacles** to our changing. Some have to do with how we deal with change in the first place: Not very well. Need predictability. Need sameness. Need to know what to expect. Need to be able to count on. Don't like surprises. Some of us get very anxious. Some of us get rattled. Some of us get angry. Addition of some sort's got us. Too hard to change. Don't want to change. Don't have to change. Don't see any reason to change. Don't know how to change. [Add your own obstacles to my list.]

There are some things in our life (when we think about it) that **we would never want to change, nor have them change**: Our love for the other. Their love for us. Our love for our children. Their love for us. Our value system. Our love for God. God's love for us. [Add what I've missed where you're concerned.]

Changing Within The Context Of
Our Primary Relationship

Since the thousands of clients I've treated over my thirty-five years as a practicing psychologist have been primarily adult couples and individuals, I'd like to confine myself to the process of changing that takes place between individuals within the context of their primary relationship.

I'd like you, my reader, therefore, to look at yourself; to look at the other; to look at how the other looks at you; to look at how you look at the other. Then ask yourself what changes you would like to see made in your relationship. Beginning with what changes you would be willing to make; then what changes you would like to see the other make.

As I have already alluded to – The one of the couple who comes to see me is usually the one most concerned with the way things are going, or not going, in their relationship.

Generally their presenting problem comes down to – They don't like the way they've been, or are being treated (or should I say mistreated). They're <u>not</u> <u>getting</u> what they <u>need</u>, or more to the point, what they <u>want</u> from the other in their relationship; and what's more, they <u>are getting</u> what they <u>don't</u> need or <u>want</u> from the other instead. What becomes evident to me, early on, is what my client's perception is of whether their other is predisposed to get involved, in any shape or form, in addressing whatever problems or concerns there may be in their relationship. Depending upon how my client perceives the other in this regard i.e. whether they perceive the other as totally unaware there may even be a problem; or whether they perceive the other as perceiving them as the one with the problem, and the other doesn't perceive themselves as having a problem, will be how I decide to proceed in helping the one who has come to see me.

If my client's other thinks there is no problem; or that it is my client who has a problem, (or is the problem) the probability there will be no couple therapy is very high. That the other may come in somewhere down the road is possible but not probable. So, my strategy then is to help my client get to the point where they'll be able to help themselves, which means helping them get stronger in all ways – mentally, emotionally, spiritually (if they're so minded) – That they then be in a much better position to make whatever changes they want to make regarding their personal growth and well being.

Therapy at this juncture focuses on improving my client's self-concept, helping them raise their self-esteem, teaching them how to be assertive especially regarding their feelings and their needs. Here is where the challenge to change comes in. Almost without exception clients who come to see me under before-mentioned circumstances need assertiveness training.

Assertiveness Holds The Key To Changing Perceptions Of Ourselves

What will teaching them to be assertive do for them if they buy into it, practice it, and don't get discouraged early on when they assert to the other, but the other's response is not what they were looking for – What do they do then, they ask me – Reassert, I tell them, and keep it up until they get a flat out "No," or an "I don't give a damn." At this point to back off makes the most sense on two counts – One, the presenter is wasting their time and energy, and the perceiver hopefully is at least hearing themselves say "No," or "I don't give a damn." There's one more important thing that my client gets out of it, i.e. at least it can't be said (it could be said but it wouldn't be true) that they didn't put it out there and that the other didn't turn them down when they did.

I want my client to change the way they look at themselves. My assumption is that their picture of themselves has been tampered with by the other. Flaws have become more prominent. Imperfections have been magnified. Irregularities have been

31

highlighted. All of these distortions a product of my client perceiving themselves as they perceive the other perceiving them.

I want my client to perceive themselves as they are becoming stronger mentally, emotionally, psychologically; more assertive of their thoughts, feelings, needs; liking the picture they see of themselves, and feeling good about it.

Will the new changing-one present themselves – not for review, which might imply they are coming before the other for their inspection and approval – but as a new changing-one who's not going to look back, but move forward, to present a self that is sure to draw the other's attention and give the other someone to be reckoned with.

It's no small thing that the one who first came to see me and plied me with a self-report of I don't likes, which mostly focused on their deteriorating relationship, and specifically upon the behaviors, (verbal and nonverbal) of the other presenting a smattering of disinterest, maltreatment and neglect, would come around to see the need for themselves to change before trying to change the other.

"Good Luck" In Changing The Other!

Can you believe you heard me say that – "before trying to change the other." Now, I've gone and done it – opening up another Pandora's Box, if you will. You thought trying to change yourself was hard enough – that's only a two on the Richter Scale..."Good Luck" in changing the other! What do I say to my client who is changing, feeling stronger, has become more assertive, and now is asking me if they may try to change the other – I put the "may" in there because by this time they trust me to such an extent that they basically are asking my permission – (That's OK with me because they are still in the dependency stage of their therapy). So we spend time talking about it first. I want to know what's going on in their head. For example, are they doing some wishful thinking. Are they fantasizing about how they'd like it to be, and so forth.

Why do we want the other to change? Let me throw some possibilities out there for you to think about. Some of us may want the other to change so that our perceptions of ourselves perceiving the other changes making it then easier for us to live with them – love them – get closer to them – and not feel that they are on our case as much – so we won't dream about being with someone else.

Others of us want the other to change because if they do we think their perception of themselves and their perception of our perception of them will change for the better.

We think the change will make things better for them because – We think they'll be happier. Feel better about themselves. Get more out of life. Get along better with others. Like themselves more. Because then we'll want to come closer and love them more and want to continue loving them. Because they could do so much more with their life. They could be much more successful in many areas. Because the kids are watching and listening and learning how to be from them.

How do we go about getting the other to change without:

Hurting their feelings

Making them angry

Pushing them away

Disturbing closeness

Giving them a complex

Making things worse

Having them turn on us

These are the kind of concerns one might have if they chance to bring up the subject of changing to the other. Caringly confronting the other about the prospect of their changing calls for a strong mind and a stout heart.

Question: Do we have the right to ask the other to change? – To act differently; to talk differently; to treat us differently? Of course we do. But what about the beam in our own eye? Let the changing begin with us. We say this. We must mean this. We must do this.

Surely there are things about ourselves we would like to change. My clients and I talk about what they would like to change about themselves. Some of these changes they would like to make have to do with their relationship. Some of them have to do just with their person. Maybe, some of the changes we make will have the desired effect on the other that we wish for. But if not, the changes will be good for us anyway. We'll be stronger and feel better about ourselves.

What Characteristics Of The Other Are Resistant To Change?

As we think about the possibility of the other changing, there come to mind characteristics of the other that are resistive to changing: stubborn; obstinate; bullheaded; narcissistic; selfish; controlling; always knows better; always thinks they're right; no one can tell them anything.

Sometimes the other comes right out with it with defenses blazing and says things that we can't believe we're hearing. What do you say to the person who says – [When you married me you knew how I was – You knew I wasn't going to change – So what's up with "I gotta change stuff?" Did you really think you could change me? Who made you the arbiter of change? Nothing you can say or do can/will make me change! Change? What's there to change? I like the way I am!]

What if we change but the other doesn't? Do we have to accept that this is the way it is and going to be? Or, do we have alternatives? How do we go about deciding what to do? Okay, the situation is this – We put it out there – How we feel – What we need – What we're willing to do to change things (Some of these changes we're already making). What's the other doing? Zippo. Nothing. The other hasn't budged an inch. It's like talking to a stone wall. Now what!

The true test of how good or bad a relationship is for you is how you feel about yourself in the presence of the other in that relationship. Think about it in this way – The better you feel about yourself when you're with the other, the better you feel about the other. The worse you feel about yourself with the other, the worse you feel about the other. Nowhere is this manifested more than if one is in a relationship with an abuser.

In a relationship with an abuser – Who, you? No way! Look for early signs. Usually the least common denominator is an inordinate need to control. Other signs: Quick to anger … easily frustrated … needs to be right … needs to have the last word … lousy listener … short on empathy … very little patience … hypercritical … judgmental … can't be told … rebels against authority … no respecter of persons … their way or the highway … rapid mood changes … carries grudges … harbors resentment … unreasonable jealousy … puts you down … belittles you … berates you … has made menacing gestures … verbal threats … throws things … destroys things … treats pets poorly … thinks of themselves first … you're always bringing up the rear … ridicules you in public, in front of your children.

What's Been Happening To You In The Company Of The Other?

Check the above out with your perceptions of your other – and then do some introspecting of your own and take a long hard objective look at yourself and see what's been, what is, happening to you – The other is dragging you down with them. You're feeling unsafe, unloved, insecure, uncomfortable. You don't like what you've become with your other. The other <u>has made you</u> – feel lousy about yourself ... feel stupid ... worthless ... dirty ... feel like a servant ... feel inferior ... feel depressed.

"Made You" – It's not a case of cause and effect, not strictly speaking. We all have a mediating ego. The other is a precipitator, increasing the probability that ... making it harder for us to feel positive about ourselves. The other has reinforced latent negative tendencies in us. Remember the situation we're talking about – one's in a relationship with an abuser. The one is changing for the better; the other either is not changing or getting worse. It takes one who has reached the point of trusting their perceptions and has had the opportunity to validate them with an objective, realistic therapist, (such as myself) and has been able to test reality by asserting their thoughts and feelings and needs to the other (about themselves and about the other) that is in a position to caringly but firmly, confront the other with the necessity for change.

"In a position to" – Meaning one with therapeutic help (It would be very hard, but not impossible, to come to this conclusion on one's own) has been able to look more objectively at one's self and look at their personality tendencies and see why it took them so long to reach this point. **See if any of these fit:** We're the eternal optimist. We could do worse. We make excuses for the other. We identify with the aggressor. We are controlled by the other. We are afraid of the other. We are guilt-prone. We have a martyr complex.

Or, **one has had thoughts like these:** I can't take it anymore. I'm tired of trying to shield the other from our problems. I can't fix this by myself. What good does it do if I change and the other doesn't. I want to give up but the other depends on me and vice versa. [(1) What can I do to help the other change? (2) How can the other help us change? (1) Nothing, if the other doesn't want, nor think they need to. (2) The other can't/won't even help themselves; how can they help us.]

Being in a position to do is, of course, not the same as doing. **Thinkers, feelers, doers** – This trichotomy represents the ways one approaches life. One way is usually primary for us. This we do first. Thus Thinkers go through their head. Feelers react with their emotions. Doers do, and think, and feel after. We wouldn't want to use anyone of these to the exclusion of the others.

Deal Breakers

I'm referring to what are one's limits or as I've said before, at what point does one say "No more" to the other. We've already gone through some of the variables involved in making that decision. For some the deal breaker could be the other's addiction – to substance, to alcohol, to, if not illegal, nevertheless, unacceptable, excessive behavior, that's taken over their life to the extent there's little or nothing left for anyone or anything else.

What to do when the other is abusing themselves – Do nothing – It's their problem. Our problem is that we're in a relationship with them. Get them help – But what do you do if they're in denial and, therefore, think they don't need any help. Or they're not in total denial, but at the same time don't want any help.

Force them, by intervention, tough love, sometimes it gets them into treatment. But, again, unless they want to change and get into actually changing and stay with it for the longer term it's not going to work.

Cajole them. Shame them. Doesn't work.

Join them. I hope you're not serious. You could end up with both of you going down the tubes.

Leave them. Now there's an extremely unhappy thought, but one certainly worth considering.

Betrayal for some is a deal-breaker. Even the thought of one's other loving another makes them sick, hurts so much, makes them angry. It's especially hurtful when the other is doing such a poor job of leaving them. Hurt debilitates, anger energizes. What's that saying? – "Don't get angry, get even"!

But what good would that do. You need to stay in control of yourself. Feel the feelings. But, then, using your head rather than your heart (with therapy) figure out what you're going to do.

For others, Living a Lie is something they can stomach no longer. It all seems so artificial, so superficial. There's no depth left in their relationship. All pretense. All pretend. All for show. One colossal cover-up. No love lost here. What once may have been, is no more. Both, long ago, stopped trying. Neither knows, for sure, who stopped first. Life in public is nothing more than a charade. In private, they don't even bother.

We've called these deal-breakers – metaphorically alluding to a juncture in our relationship when all bets are off. There will be no more wheeling and dealing. We want off the train to nowhere. Thinking, feeling, doing. The doing part is the one some have the most problems with.

Giving The Other An Ultimatum, What Makes It So Hard?

When we reflect upon our particular situation, we might be wondering what took us so long to reach this point that we're ready to give the other an ultimatum. Consider these possibilities – We might put these in the category of what makes it so hard for one to get away and/or stay away from the other abusing them: Poor self-concept. Low self-esteem. Too large a caretaking need. Think we deserve what we get. For better or for worse. Dependent, financially, emotionally. We were abused as children. We made our bed, now we're sleeping in it. We're in denial. We're hoping the other will change. The other knows what buttons to push. The other can't help it. The other flip-flops, good – bad – good – bad.

What Do You Do? (The One Giving The Ultimatum)

Arrange for a time and place, when and where it works for both of you. A private place where you're alone with minimal distractions – Unless you're afraid for yourself because the other's past behaviors have made you fearful of their reactions. And say: I want to talk to you and I want you just to listen to what I have to say and don't interrupt me. When I'm done, I'm willing to listen to what you have to say in return. First of all, I want you to know that I still love you, and that makes it even harder to say what I 'm going to say to you. I love you but I don't like your behavior. I don't like the way you treat me. I love you but I don't like what you've become and the way you are. I don't like the way I feel about you when we interact. I don't like the way I feel about me when I'm with you. My love for you is fading; it's getting weaker. I don't like the feeling that I'm losing my love for you. I don't want my love for you to die.

But here's the thing that bothers me most about our situation. I feel I've been doing my part to change whatever I need to change to make our relationship better. I've been going to therapy so that I can better understand myself and have a better understanding of what's happening to us.

Now, it's your turn: I'm trying to change and grow; but I don't see you doing any changing. I came to the conclusion that I couldn't change on my own, that I needed help to change. It wasn't easy for me to make the decision to get help. My first thought was that I should be able to do this on my own. Now I know differently and I don't feel weaker but stronger for seeking help.

I know I'm me and you're you. But we're us. And us is not going to make it unless we both get help to change and grow. I've approached you before about getting help; and you've said I'll think about it, but then did nothing about it. Maybe you were hoping I'd forget, that time would pass and maybe things would get better between us by themselves. Didn't happen did it! So it's time to get serious, really serious. I know how you feel about being told, about being ordered to do something. Well, this is not an order I'm giving you. It's a choice. I'd like you to see it that way. But that will be up to you.

Either – Or. The choice comes down to this. Either you get professional help or I'm leaving you (We're done, finished, finis).

This is It! Before you think there's someone else, there isn't. I still love you, but not as you are, not how you treat me (mistreat me) mistreat yourself. If you don't get help to change and get into the process of changing, I'm choosing not to live with you anymore.

What The Other Needs To Do

You assert a reasonable timetable. The other should make their own appointment (Don't do it for them). When I am the therapist seeing the one who's given the other an ultimatum, and they've been with me for several sessions, I would not be willing to work with the other given the ultimatum. The reason for this is that I'm the therapist of record for the one – The other, if I took them on, would likely perceive me and the one I'm treating in a collusion, and that it was two against one (Which it wouldn't be of course, but what's in the eye of the perceiver is real to them).

So the other should make their own appointment with a therapist other than the one their other is seeing and go alone the first time. If their therapist wants to see the other, the other should be willing to go, once, so the other's therapist can get a first-hand perception of them. After this one time seeing the other's therapist, the other is on their own. It works best for each to have their own therapist. If eventually you both want to work on your relationship together, find a third therapist.

51

An alternative would be that you go together the first time. But you must find a therapist who is willing and able to work with you individually and collectively. If the therapist is not willing to work this way, but will see you only as a couple, find one who is willing and able, or go the way of my first suggestion.

Okay so here's the situation – You've been in therapy and still are. The other now has a therapist of their own. Now what? You're the one who gave the other an ultimatum. You wait and see, but you <u>don't put your life on hold</u>. You keep doing what you've been doing. You don't back up. You may back off a little, but you don't want to present the perception that all is well now that the other's in therapy. For goodness sakes, <u>continue your therapy</u>, which, as it should, focuses on you – giving you insights about yourself and the other, More assertiveness training reinforcing you to stay in charge of yourself, giving you an objective, realistic therapist with whom to validate your perceptions of yourself and the other.

The One Getting The Ultimatum, What Is It Like For Them

If I were treating the one who was given the ultimatum, I would expect to see at first, someone who is presenting themselves under duress behaving like someone having no choice in the control of the other.

For one who is used to being in control, doing, saying what they like, behaving the way they feel like behaving – out of control of themselves at times while trying to control the other – coming to therapy to be assessed and evaluated (at least that's how they see it) is a bitter pill to swallow.

But they're here. That tells me something, which I relate back to them. It tells me (I tell them) that they don't want to lose the other, that they're afraid the other is going to leave them or ask them to leave. Or if they're further along in their introspection they are feeling badly about where things have come to between they and the other.

What Are They Like If They're Starting To Get It?

If in our earlier sessions they are able to move away from feeling sorry for themselves, or blaming the other for triggering their bad behavior and are beginning to be accountable and take responsibility for their abusive behavior and the perception of themselves they gave to the other, their prognosis is fair to good (at least from their perspective). They are starting to get it. They are starting to see themselves as the other has seen them and they don't like what they see. Seeing ourselves as we see others see us is not a pretty sight.

Good thing, that it isn't a pretty sight to the one who got the ultimatum. This tells me that they're lowering their defenses and seeing things the way they really are – the way the other has seen them and would continue to see them unless and until they change.

The assumption I'm making now is both the one who gave the ultimatum and the other who got it are now in therapy working hard with their respective therapists and that they are in couple therapy with a third perceptually neutral therapist. Keep in mind, however, that even though the therapeutic setup may be ideal, changes in their personalities and in their presentation to each other and their perceptions of each other depend on whether what they learn about themselves (as individuals and as a couple, from the insights given them) they are able to convert into observable behavioral change.

What Is The One Who Gave The Ultimatum Looking For From The Other?

The one who was given the ultimatum and responded by getting help will want to include in their repertoire of behavioral changes: – Taking ownership for their abusive behavior. Putting this taking responsibility for the same into so many words to the other. Saying they're sorry for having been so mean and hurtful with their words and acts. Then promising to curtail, diminish, and ultimately extinguish such behavior.

But, as you probably noticed, all of this is <u>just words</u> at this point, sounding like they are sincerely meant. But, again, keep in mind behavioral change involves not only changing verbally, but non-verbally as well. By their actions one shall know them.

The one who issued the ultimatum is asking themselves, is this enough to forgive them and get past the situation. Needing more than this from the other would certainly be effected by how many times they may have heard variations of this before. To make true believers of them, they would have to see consistency over time in demonstrable behavioral change i.e. a substantial reduction, if not extinction, of before-perpetrated-abusive behavior (If abusive behavior had had a <u>physical</u> component, there would be no, "one more time").

When Is Enough Not Enough?

Extinction or near extinction of old behavioral patterns is not enough nor should be enough to verify that the other is changing. New behaviors, a new tone to their way of speaking that conveys closeness rather than control would need to be forthcoming. Essentially the new behaviors would be replacing the old behaviors. Simplistically, it would be like the one who was given the ultimatum getting in touch with the other side of themselves – In some instances, perceiving themselves as they behaved before and turning this completely around. For example, the taker becomes the giver; the one who believed to need-is-to-be-weak, now knows what they need to be strong and come through for their other with tender strength.

What If The One Giving The Ultimatum Gets A <u>No Way</u> From The Other?

Having worked with many a client who has finally become strong enough to give the other an ultimatum, I know from their experience that it hasn't always turned out the way I've been describing. With some, their other has balked and stalled. With some, the other has said, <u>No way</u>, I'm not going to get any help. I don't need any help. You're the one with the problem. You're the one who needs help. With some, the other has said, There's the door, or, I'm out of here.

If you're the one who is giving the other an ultimatum, you never know ahead of time how they'll react. The important thing is that you stay strong, in control of yourself. Hopefully, you (before this) have gotten help for yourself and that help continues and regardless of the other's response you will remain resolute and move forward.

If you're the one getting the ultimatum, I hope you will be able to listen to what the other is saying to you, <u>really</u> saying to you, and that your defenses will not be so high that nothing will get through. I hope you'll be able to see yourself for the moment as the other is presenting you with how they see you. That your defenses don't find it necessary to completely shield you from the reality of what the other is perceiving and presenting and that you're then able and at least reluctantly willing to seek help for your sake as well as the sake of the other.

As A Therapist I Wish Both Had Come To Me Sooner

If I had my druthers, of course, I would prefer if people came to see me long before they have reached the point of giving or getting an ultimatum. I'd like to think with my help we could nip this thing in the bud. Especially do I think I could help them if they came to see me as a couple who wanted things to change in their relationship – Each had needs that the other wasn't addressing. Each didn't like things about the other's behavior. Each was perceiving in the other's presentation i.e. in their facial expression, gestures, how they said, what they said, personality characteristics that were turning them off, pushing them away, keeping them at bay, hurting their feelings, making them angry, verbally, emotionally, psychologically – coming very close to – if not there already, abusing them.

Getting to my clients before there's an ultimatum, I have to say makes my work a heck of a lot easier and I have to say makes it a lot more probable that their relationship can be repaired. The earlier they come to see me the better: – We're talking when either one is sensing something's wrong. Things are not clicking. There's a distance growing between them. They're losing their friendship. Feelings for the other are not as strong as they once were. They're less tolerant of the other's foibles. They're losing some respect, both ways. [It's time to follow your senses. Talk about what you're perceiving and how you're feeling and what you're needing – each of you to the other. It could very well be that the other was sensing the same things as you.]

Maybe, you'll be able to talk it through, each of you letting the other know what you need that you're not getting. Try to do this in a non-blaming way. Try to receive this in a non-defensive way. If you can come to an understanding and are able to negotiate a compromise that is reciprocal and commit to it you're truly on your way to repairing tears in your relationship before they get larger.

If you're not able to get there the first attempt, keep yourselves open to further dialogue. Don't give up asserting and listening. Reinforce whatever behavioral changes for the better you see in yourself or the other. Try not to overreact to regressive behaviors on either part. A slip doesn't necessarily signal a slide.

If you decide you personally could use some help to figure out what your part is in all of this, go for it, seek therapy. You personally deserve to be happy and have a relationship in which you can grow yourself and help the other grow. Your other does as well, but it will be up to the other to decide whether they personally want to go the therapy route. Hopefully the other will for their sake and yours and the relationship you hold so dear.

The Saddest Scenario Of All

I've saved the saddest scenario for the last. One gives the ultimatum; one sets a timetable for the other. It comes and goes and nothing happens. The ball is now back in the one's court. **Of course, it will be up to you.** No therapist should be instructing you what to do. Assuming you have your own therapist working with you, they are there to support you in whatever decision you make. I'm sure they will run by you the realities they perceive in your situation, together with you weigh the plusses and minuses, the costs versus rewards. But whatever you decide they'll stick with you to see you through ramifications of whatever you choose to do. [I guess I shouldn't be speaking for other therapists, but I sure as heck would.]

If one decides to leave or have the other leave after the ultimatum has run its course to no avail, then one will continue to need therapeutic support to stay on track and see this through. If one thought they could do this but now it's turning out they're waffling they certainly need therapeutic support all the more. Because they are now in the throes of a conflict (avoidance – avoidance, probably, since either way has negatives). Such a conflict generates much anxiety. To get off of dead center one may resort to their defenses, in particular, the defense of rationalization.

Rationalization As A Defense

In this particular situation the defense would work this way – Remember, in point of time, <u>one</u> has already perceived the other doing nothing about the ultimatum and the ultimatum's time has expired. The <u>other</u> who was given the ultimatum in reality is the same person <u>before</u> and <u>after</u> the ultimatum. If the other in some way is now looking better to the one who gave the ultimatum, it's fair to suspect that the defense of rationalization is working hard to reduce the anxiety generated by the conflict. I call this "sweet lemon rationalization" in that the other once perceived a "lemon" is now perceived as somehow sweeter. If this is what I see to be the case – that my client, who is in the particular situation I've alluded to, is employing this particular defense, I don't try to take it from them. But I do try to get them to lower it so they can begin once again to see things about their other the way they are and not how their defenses present the other to be. Remember, if you end up so conflicted, and you're waffling – even though anxiety is growing (If you're in therapy, good; if not, get in it pronto), you need to lower your defenses; then trust your perceptions; validate them with your therapist. Then, only then, **Choose to do what's going to be good for you.**

You owe this to yourself as a person of great worth.

My Message To You My Reader

My message to you my reader is to be aware, be perceptive, early on, of things you don't like (along with things you do like, of course). Pay attention to how this social personal exchange you have with the other is panning out, i.e. costs versus rewards. Assert early on what you need. Don't be brushed aside, avoided or ignored. Have respect for yourself. Respect should be reciprocal, as should caring, nurturing, supporting, trusting. If not, why not! What's going on that you're not getting these from the other; nor do you feel like (and therefore you may not be) giving them to the other.

Your relationship is not something to be lightly regarded nor taken for-granted. It is to be given a very high priority in the scheme of things. Take good care of it. Do not count on it to take care of itself. And for goodness sakes, don't you let it get to the point where it becomes necessary to give or receive an ultimatum. Better late than never, maybe; but I wouldn't take that chance if you can help it.

Blessings

Take Good Care,

Doc Ken

K. L. Fischer, PhD

DON'T LIKE THE WAY IT IS? CHANGE IT!

About the Author

- Dr. Kenneth L. Fischer (affectionately called Doc Ken) has been in helping professions his entire adult life.

- Founder and pastor of Peace Lutheran Church, Disco, MI

- Pastor of Mt. Olive Lutheran Church, Grand Rapids, MI

- Junior High School teacher 8th grade English, 9th grade Latin, Muskego, MI

- First psychologist in the history of the Men's Unit, State Prison, Lowell, FL

- Dr. Fischer received his PhD in Personality Psychology, Michigan State University, East Lansing, MI

- His doctoral work was in Person Perception

- An instructor and lecturer, Dept. of Psychology, University of Wisconsin, Milwaukee, WI

- Also taught at various colleges throughout the Milwaukee-Metro area, namely Milwaukee Area Technical College, Mt. Mary College, Alverno College, and at Carthage College, Racine, WI

- Dr. Fischer has been a practicing psychologist in his own clinic for the past thirty-five years, treating adult couples and individuals

- ☐ His areas of expertise are in Personality and Person Perception

- ☐ His specialty is Personality Disorders

- ☐ Support Therapy Clinic is located in Hartland, WI

Other Books by Kenneth L. Fischer, PhD

Closeness Without Control:
The Key To A Loving Reciprocal Relationship Of
Assertive Independent Equals

Seeing Ourselves As We See Others See Us:
Our Personality Develops Through Person Perception
and Self-Experience

The Gray Area Of Psychological Abuse:
Abusee? Abuser? Or Both? How Can We Tell?
What Can We Do?

**Psychologically Speaking What Are We
Really Saying?**
The Music Behind The Music Behind Our Words

We've Got Personality!
Now What?

Don't Be A Stranger (To Yourself):
Go Outside Yourself To Get Inside Yourself Then Turn
Yourself Inside Out

**The Art And Efficacy Of Managing Person
Perceptions:**
Manipulation In Its Highest Psychotherapeutic Sense

In Defense Of Defensiveness:
Knowing Our Defenses, Lowering Our Defenses,
Living With Our Defenses

The Incomparable Spunkerface and Company:
Heaven Sent - Heaven Bent

Lamenting The Loss of Loyalty:
Where Has All The Loyalty Gone?!